29. 6. 2007.

Especially for . . .

Carol.

Best Wishes

in your new

home

Regards

Rima.

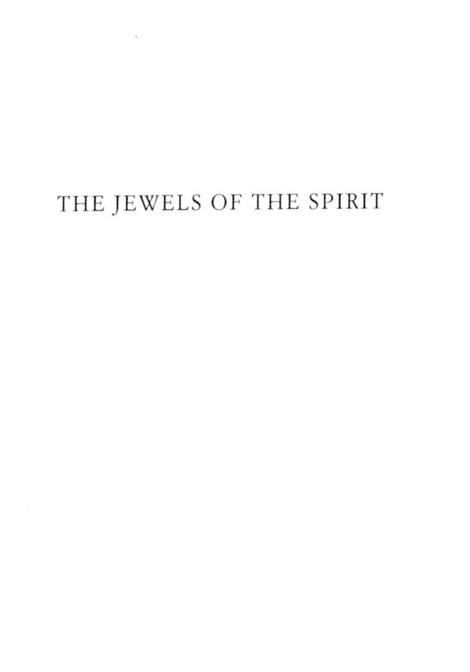

THE JEWELS OF THE SPIRIT

Written AND Illustrated

BY

JOAN WALSH ANGLUND

Andrews McMeel Publishing

Kansas City

 For information, write Andrews McMeel Publishing, an Andrews McMeel Universal company, 4520 Main Street, Kansas City, Missouri 64111.

www.andrewsmcmeel.com

ISBN: 0-8362-6789-3

Library of Congress Catalog Card Number: 98-84164

Dedicated to Deborah Harrison

Gladness

is the trumpet

of the Spirit!

Reason's

farthest reach

can only

touch the hem

of Faith's

fair garments.

Heaven

lies within you.

You carry it

with you . . .

wherever you go!

Only Love

can lift us

to our true purpose

here.

Collect not

the things

of this world.

Rather,

leave them behind

. . . as a child's

outgrown toys,

and

gather, instead,

the Jewels of the Spirit.

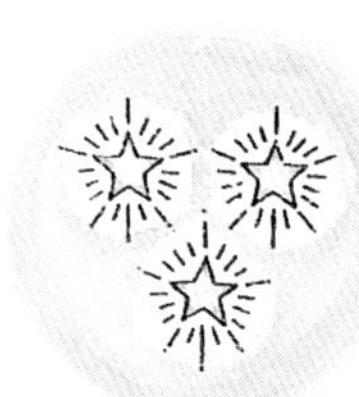

Every star

is made brighter

by the darkness

surrounding it.

The brave-hearted

have as many problems

as others

. . . they but

face them

differently.

What lovely things

begin

. . . because

someone

cares!

The bravest smile
often hides
a broken heart.

Many truths

are found

in solitude

that

hide

. . . when others come.

Hope,

like a candle within,

burns

steadily

. . . through every storm.

Faith is the staff

that will support you

over the rockiest terrain.

Let my heart

be quick

to Love

. . . and slow

to judge.

Release

oft brings

a needed

Peace.

We dwell

in shadow

or

in sunlight

. . . according

to our

belief.

We carry the Past

with us.

No matter how fast

or how far

we may travel,

like our luggage,

It arrives

with us

. . . at every destination!

Though

the Rose

is plucked

. . . the Root

remains.

Often

kindness succeeds

where anger

would fail.

By our choices

. . . we are revealed.

A dream

is a festival

of lights

within your mind.

The blowing winds

of Time

carry us to lands

we never expected

to see.

We must forgive

the Past

before

we can be free

to embrace

the Future.

Our Faith

grows stronger

with

our every prayer.

Tears,

like a tender rain,

can cleanse

the landscape

of the soul.

The best way

to help yourself

is

to help someone

else.

All the strength

of darkness

cannot stop

a single dawn.

The simplest delights

in Life

are, often,

. . . the sweetest.

Daily,

we must cleanse

our spirit

of discontent

and doubt,

as we would

wash a garment

clean

of the stains

of yesterday.

Your strength lies

. . . in your Hope.

Your salvation lies

. . . in your Faith.

Let us climb, together,

to the hilltop . . .

the Sun

is still shining

there.

Every small spring bud

teaches

that we, too,

have the power

to "begin" again.

Our mistakes

can be turned

into victories

. . . if we will learn

from them.

The mind

is a patient spider

. . . ever weaving

gossamer webs

of fantasy and hope.

Every hour

. . . an Opportunity!

Every instant

. . . a Gift!

We can only help someone

when that person

is ready to be helped.

No Evil

can stain

the heart

that is

Pure.

How beautiful

is our world

. . . if we will just

lift our eyes

to see it!

Life is in the living.

Love is in the giving.

In a garden

. . . all is Beauty!

Time

has no power

here.

Sometimes we find

our truth

so casually.

But

it was always there,

waiting . . .

hidden by the cloaking curtain

of daily events.

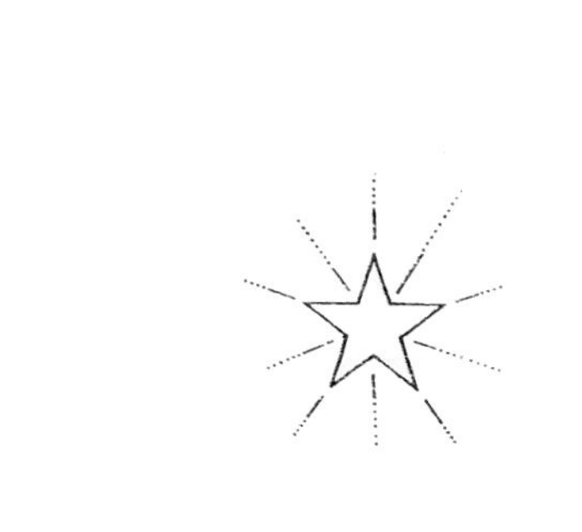

Each soul

is a star

in the great universe

of Spirit.

What exquisite music

is ours

. . . when we listen

to Nature's

sweet murmurs.

If we would have

our share

of Joy

. . . we must, first,

learn to give it.

Faith

gives us

the Power

to be strong.

To Love

is our true purpose

here

. . . nothing else matters.